THE CHILDREN'S BOOK OF Saints & Angels

Claire Llewellyn

KINGFISHER
LONDON & NEW YORK

KINGFISHER
LONDON & NEW YORK

First published in 2003
This updated edition published in 2026 in the United States by Kingfisher
120 Broadway, New York, NY 10271
Kingfisher is an imprint of Macmillan Children's Books, London

2003 edition:
Consultant: Annette Reynolds at AD Publishing Services
2026 edition:
Editor: Daisy Edwards
Senior designer: Lisa Sodeau
Additional text: Laura Gilbert

ISBN 978-0-7534-8165-3

Kingfisher books are available for special promotions and premiums.
For details contact: Special Markets Department, Macmillan,
120 Broadway, New York, NY 10271

Printed in China
9 8 7 6 5 4 3 2 1
1TR/1225/WKT/UG

EU representative: Macmillan Publishers Ireland Ltd, 1st Floor,
The Liffey Trust Centre, 117-126 Sheriff Street Upper,
Dublin 1 D01 YC43

Distributed in the U.S. and Canada by Macmillan,
120 Broadway, New York, NY 10271

Library of Congress Cataloging-in-Publication data has been applied for.

MIX
Paper | Supporting responsible forestry
FSC® C116313

Acknowledgements
The publishers would like to thank the following for supplying photographs for this book:
b = bottom, c = center, l = left, t = top, r = right
Cover (front): The Picture Art Collection/Alamy. Cover (back): (t) Peter Horree/Alamy; (cl) jozef sedmak/Alamy; (cr) Zvonimir Atletic/Shutterstock; (bl) fatimadesigner/Shutterstock; (br) usmanify/Shutterstock.
Interiors: 1, 3, 6, 8c, 10, 19t, 22t, 28t, 30t 30b, 31t, 36, 38t, 39t, 42r, 45t, 50r and 50b Renata Sedmakova/Shutterstock; 4b Marco Iacobucci Epp /Shutterstock; 4r fotogiunta/Shutterstock; 5 Peter Horree/Alamy; 7 Photo12/Ann Ronan Picture Library/Alamy; 8b Joan Sutter/Shutterstock; 9t duncan1890/iStock Images; 9b and 29t PaoloGaetano/iStock Images; 10, 14, 16, 20b, 22b, 41 and 55 sedmak/iStock Images; 11 TerryHealy/iStock Images; 12 supersizer/iStock Images; 13 dmitriymoroz/iStock Images; 15 Jesus_Higueras_Foto/Shutterstock; 17 and 18t The Picture Art Collection/Alamy; 18 hxdbzxy/Shutterstock; 19b Saharat Thinagun/Shutterstock; 21t duncan1890/GettyImages; 21bl and 56 ZU_09/iStock Images; 23t Zvonimir Atletic/Shutterstock; 23b Grafissimo/iStock Images; 24 Lanmas/Alamy; 25 Irene Miller/Shutterstock; 26t, 35 and 43t Heritage Images/GettyImages; 26b essevu/Shutterstock; 27t Paolo Romiti/Alamy; 27b RobNaw/Shutterstock; 28b godongphoto/Shutterstock; 29b fatimadesigner/Shutterstock; 31b Manfred13/Shutterstock; 32 Cynthia Liang/Shutterstock; 33 Joaquin Ossorio Castillo/Shutterstock; 34 Frame Stock Footage/Shutterstock; 37 Sanit Fuangnakhon/Shutterstock; 38b Zvonimir Atletic/Shutterstock; 39b and 45b PeopleImages/Shutterstock; 40l usmanify/Shutterstock; 40r Shahi Malik/Shutterstock; 41 Photo Beto/iStock Images; 42b GSDesign/Shutterstock; 43b encierro/Shutterstock; 44t MireXa/iStock Images; 44b New Africa/Shutterstock; 46t jorisvo/Shutterstock; 46b Robert Clay/Alamy; 47t Christopher Furlong/GettyImages; 47b evgeeenius/Shutterstock; 48 and 51r ZU_09/GettyImages; 49 TerryJLawrence/iStock Images; 51b agutsavop/iStock Images; 52 goga18128/Shutterstock; 53 Zvonimir Atletic/Shutterstock; 54 Science History Images/Alamy; 57 jozef sedmak/Alamy; 58 Heritage Image Partnership Ltd/Alamy; 59 ArtMari/Shutterstock.

Contents

What is a saint?

Feast Day: November 1 (All Saints' Day)

The name "saint" is given to a Christian person who has died and is worthy of great honor and respect. The name comes from the Latin word *sanctus*, meaning holy.

The first people to be made saints were Christ's family, his apostles, and the early Christian martyrs in the first century. These people were very well-known and became saints by word of mouth. The saints were given a feast day–a day of celebration that fell on the anniversary of their death rather than their birth. After all, death was the moment when the saints were taken into heaven.

There are many thousands of saints from all walks of life including peasants, princesses, teachers, soldiers, writers, doctors.

WITH THE PASSING CENTURIES, IT WAS LESS EASY TO DECIDE WHO WAS WORTHY OF BEING A SAINT. EVENTUALLY, IN 1170, THE POPE DECIDED THAT HE SHOULD APPROVE ALL NEW SAINTS IN A PROCESS CALLED CANONIZATION. THIS IS STILL HOW PEOPLE BECOME SAINTS TODAY.

Most saints had a special gift—of loving God, of caring for the needy, of healing or teaching, of patience and wisdom.

Some saints traveled and did good deeds; others started religious houses and lived lives of simplicity and prayer. While some saints' lives are little more than legend, others are all too real. Many of the early saints faced persecution, torture, and a brutal death.

For many Christians, the saints play an important role. They were once human, just like us, with human weaknesses and fears. Now that they are in heaven, close to God, they may act as valuable go-betweens, watching over us, protecting us, caring, and praying for us. The saints in this book led extraordinary lives. Most of them faced enormous problems and met death with courage and faith. As some of the world's most inspiring role models, they can show us how to be better people.

The Forerunners of Christ with Saints and Martyrs
by Fra Angelico, The National Gallery, London, UK

Virgin Mary

Feast Day: August 15

Mary is the most important of all the saints—a person so good and holy that she was chosen to be the mother of God's own son. Mary loved Jesus and, in spite of her trust in God, suffered greatly as she watched him die.

Mary lived in Nazareth, Galilee. She was a gentle young woman who was engaged to a carpenter called Joseph. One day the archangel Gabriel visited her and told her that she would have a baby who would be the Son of God. Mary was amazed.

Mary was God's servant, and would do as he wished.

When the baby was due, Mary and Joseph traveled to Bethlehem to register for their taxes. The town was so busy that they had to stay in a stable, where Jesus was born. Mary was overjoyed at her baby boy and, weeks later she took him to the temple and dedicated him to God.

Mary loved Jesus with all her heart. As he grew up, she saw how special he was. She was with him when he performed his first miracle. They were at a wedding when the wine ran out, so Jesus changed jars of water into wine!

MARY KNEW THAT JESUS WAS DOING GOD'S WORK ON EARTH AND SHE SUFFERED WITH HIM AS HE DIED ON THE CROSS. MARY KNEW ABOUT JESUS' ASCENSION INTO HEAVEN. MANY CHRISTIANS BELIEVE THAT SHE, TOO, WAS TAKEN INTO HEAVEN. SHE IS THE PATRON SAINT OF ALL HUMANITY AND NUMEROUS THINGS ACROSS DIFFERENT CULTURES AND TRADITIONS.

Crucifixion by Karl Geiger, Vienna, Austria

The *Madonna of Humility* by Lippo di Dalmasio, The National Gallery, London, UK

St. Joseph

Feast Day: March 19

Joseph was the husband of Mary, the mother of Jesus. Joseph was the protector of the Holy Family. Although he wasn't Jesus' birth father, he loved and taught the young boy as if he were his own son.

Joseph felt responsible for the Holy Family and always did his best to protect them.

The St. Joseph by Josef Kastner, Vienna, Austria

Joseph, a carpenter from Nazareth, was engaged to Mary. He was an honest, respectable man. He must have been surprised when Mary told him she was expecting a baby and amazed when an angel explained that the baby was the Son of God! Joseph found the stable where Jesus was born. He hurried the family to safety in Egypt after an angel warned him that King Herod was planning to murder all baby boys.

IT IS THOUGHT THAT JOSEPH MUST HAVE DIED WHILE JESUS WAS STILL YOUNG. HE WAS NOT THERE WHEN JESUS WAS CRUCIFIED. ST. JOSEPH IS KNOWN AS THE PATRON SAINT OF MANY THINGS, INCLUDING CARPENTERS, THE CHURCH, FATHERS OF FAMILIES, AND SOCIAL JUSTICE.

Stained glass, Paris, France

St. Anne

Feast Day: July 26

The legend of St. Anne tells how, after years of being childless, a holy woman had a daughter called Mary and became grandmother to the baby Jesus.

There are no historical facts known about Anne, but in the early centuries of Christianity, a story grew. She was said to be married to a man named Joachim, who lived in Nazareth. After 20 years of marriage, the couple had no children. Joachim decided to go into the desert for 40 days and 40 nights to pray for a child. While he was away, Anne was visited by an angel, who told her that God had heard their prayers and that they would have a child.

Engraving of Saint Anne

Anne was so grateful when her daughter, Mary, was born, that she dedicated her to God.

ANNE'S LEGEND TELLS US THAT SHE LOVINGLY RAISED MARY TO PUT HER TRUST AND FAITH IN GOD. ANNE WAS DEVOTED TO HER GRANDSON, JESUS. ST. ANNE IS THE PATRON SAINT OF CANADA, GRANDMOTHERS, PREGNANT WOMEN, AND MANY OTHER THINGS TOO.

Detail of mosaic, Umbria, Italy

St. John the Baptist by Rodolfo Morgari,
Turin, Italy

St. John the Baptist

Feast day: June 24

John the Baptist was a prophet who prepared people for the coming of a great leader called the Messiah.

John was son of Zechariah and Elizabeth, Mary's cousin. One day, John was visited by the archangel Gabriel, who told him that his wife would have a son who would become a prophet—a messenger of God.

John grew into a remarkable man. To prepare for life as a prophet, he lived in the desert for years. John became a powerful preacher, and huge crowds gathered to hear him speak. He told them to prepare for the arrival of the Messiah, a leader promised by God. He urged them to confess their sins and be baptized in the Jordan River. One day Jesus came to be baptized.

John recognized Jesus instantly—he was the Messiah!

John was fearless and outspoken. When King Herod Antipas married his brother's wife, Herodias, John protested and was sent to prison. Herodias hated John and wanted him dead. Her daughter, Salome, danced for Herod and was offered a gift in return. Salome, acting on her mother's behalf, asked for John's head. The order went out, and the prophet was beheaded.

ST. JOHN THE BAPTIST IS THE PATRON SAINT OF MANY THINGS, INCLUDING BAPTISM. HE IS KNOWN FOR BAPTIZING PEOPLE AND PREPARING THEM FOR JESUS. BAPTISMS STILL TAKE PLACE TODAY AS PART OF WELCOMING PEOPLE INTO THE CHRISTIAN FAITH.

St. Mary Magdalene

Feast day: July 22

Mary Magdalene was a devoted friend of Jesus and was with him when he died. Days later her sorrow turned to joy as she became the first person to see him rise from the dead.

Mary Magdalene lived in a small town by the Sea of Galilee. She suffered from a horrible illness caused by seven devils, but she was cured by Jesus when he visited her town. She was baptized a Christian, and became his devoted follower. She was with Jesus at his crucifixion and stayed with him until the moment he died.

Two days later Mary and some other women went to the tomb to anoint Jesus' body with perfumes and spices. They found the tomb empty, with the huge stone that was blocking the entrance rolled away.

Mary, heartbroken, wept by the tomb.

Soon a man came up to comfort her. When he gently spoke her name, she realized it was Jesus!

He told her to go and tell his disciples that he had risen from the dead.

With her heart full of joy, Mary ran to Jesus' friends to tell them the good news.

MARY MAGDALENE IS KNOWN AS THE PATRON SAINT OF PEOPLE WHO ARE SORRY AND SEEK FORGIVENESS—THOSE WHO WANT TO IMPROVE AND START AFRESH. SHE MAY BE SEEN AS A FIGURE OF SUPPORT AND TRANSFORMATION.

Fresco of Saint Mary Magdalene by Piero della Francesca, Tuscany, Italy.

Fresco of St. Peter the Apostle by Josef Kastner, Vienna, Austria

St. Peter the Apostle

Feast Day: June 29

Peter was a fisherman who loved and followed Jesus. Peter is probably the best known of all the disciples, and became not only their leader but the leader of the Christian church.

Peter, first known as Simon, lived near the Sea of Galilee. One day, as he and his brother Andrew were fishing, Jesus asked them to follow him. Jesus gave Simon the name Peter, which means "rock", saying that he was the rock on which God's church would be built.

Peter was always at Jesus' side, and he saw him perform many miracles. When Peter and the disciples were in a boat on the stormy waters of the Sea of Galilee, they saw Jesus walking across the water. Peter, an eager, warmhearted man, jumped out of the boat to meet his master and found that he, too, could walk on the water! But he panicked and began to sink until Jesus came to his aid.

Jesus loved Peter and saw a great strength in him.

But sometimes the disciple let Jesus down. One night Peter denied knowing Jesus and deserted him after his arrest. After the resurrection Jesus forgave Peter and asked him to lead his church.

PETER TRAVELED, TELLING PEOPLE ABOUT JESUS. WITH GOD'S HELP, PETER PERFORMED MIRACLES. HE ARRIVED IN ROME AT A TIME WHEN CHRISTIANS WERE PERSECUTED AND, IN ABOUT AD 64, PETER WAS ARRESTED AND CRUCIFIED. HIS TOMB IS SAID TO LIE AT ST. PETER'S BASILICA IN THE VATICAN IN ROME. HE IS KNOWN, AMONG MANY THINGS, AS THE PATRON SAINT OF ROME AND OF FISHERMEN.

St. Paul the Apostle

Feast Day: June 29

After years spent persecuting Christians, Paul had a blinding vision and was converted to Christianity. He was one of the most important missionaries and founders of the Christian church.

Paul, first called Saul, was a Roman citizen who had been taught by the Greeks. He was also a Jew who followed his religion strictly. He had never met Jesus and did not believe he was the Messiah. Saul did not like the Christians, and he had many of them arrested. He wanted to stamp out this new religion.

One day, when riding to the city of Damascus, Saul was blinded by a light. He heard the voice of Jesus ask why he was persecuting Jesus. Saul was led into Damascus where, three days later, Jesus restored his sight. Saul realized that Jesus was the Messiah, and was baptized. From that day, he was known as Paul.

Paul became a great preacher and writer, and an important missionary.

He traveled tirelessly for many years, performing miracles and spreading the word of Jesus. He wrote letters to his new Christian groups, offering encouragement and advice.

ALTHOUGH OFTEN IN TROUBLE, HURT, AND IMPRISONED, PAUL NEVER LOST HIS FAITH. ST. PAUL IS THE PATRON SAINT OF MISSIONARIES, WRITERS, TENT MAKERS, AND MANY OTHER THINGS. HE IS OFTEN SHOWN HOLDING A BOOK AND A SWORD. WE ESPECIALLY REMEMBER ST. PAUL ON JUNE 29TH, THE SAME DAY AS ST. PETER.

St. Paul the Apostle, unknown artist, Italy

Conversion of St Paul on the Road to Damascus by Hans Speckaert, Paris, France

St. Andrew

Feast Day: November 30

Andrew was one of Jesus' 12 disciples and also one of his closest friends. Less well-known than his brother, Peter, Andrew followed Jesus all his life, and, like him, he died on a cross.

Andrew was a fisherman and a follower of John the Baptist. When John said that Jesus was the Messiah, Andrew believed him. Jesus saw Andrew and his brother fishing and asked them to be his disciples. Andrew answered Jesus' call and urged Peter to join him.

Andrew saw Jesus perform many miracles.

One day Jesus was preaching to a crowd of people who were very hungry. Andrew found a boy with five loaves of bread and two fish. Jesus miraculously used this to feed more than 5,000 people!

The Crucifixion of St. Andrew by a Master of the Murano Gradual, origin Venice, Italy

IT IS THOUGHT THAT ANDREW BECAME A MISSIONARY AND WAS CRUCIFIED ON AN X-SHAPED CROSS. IT IS SAID THAT HE PREACHED FOR TWO DAYS BEFORE HE DIED. JUST LIKE HIS BROTHER (ST. PETER), ST. ANDREW IS THE PATRON SAINT OF FISHERMEN. HE IS ALSO THE PATRON SAINT OF GREECE, RUSSIA, SCOTLAND, AND MANY OTHER PLACES AROUND THE WORLD.

St. Thomas

Feast Day: July 3

The disciple Thomas found it so hard to believe that Jesus had risen from the dead that, almost 2,000 years after his own death, he is still known as "Doubting Thomas."

After Jesus rose from the dead, he appeared to his disciples–but Thomas was not there. Later, when Thomas heard the amazing news, he could not believe it. He stated he wanted to see and touch the marks on Jesus' hands before believing.

Poor Thomas must have felt ashamed when he saw Jesus.

His master invited him to touch his wounds. Jesus gently forgave Thomas.

Not much more is known about Thomas. It believed he was killed with a spear.

The Doubt of St. Thomas, unknown artist, Turin, Italy

ST. THOMAS IS SAID TO HAVE BEEN A MISSIONARY IN INDIA. HE IS KNOWN AS THE PATRON SAINT OF INDIA AND OF PAKISTAN. HE IS ALSO DESCRIBED, AMONG OTHER THINGS, AS THE PATRON SAINT OF ARCHITECTS, DUE TO HIS SKILLS AS A BUILDER.

St. Matthew

Feast Day: September 21

Once hated as a tax collector, Matthew became one of Jesus' disciples. He is best known as the writer of the first book of the New Testament—the Gospel according to St. Matthew.

Matthew, who lived in Galilee, was a tax collector. Tax collectors were shunned by people and were banned from some temple services. The fact that the taxes went to the Romans made matters worse. In spite of this, Jesus called on Matthew to become one of his most trusted friends.

Fresco of St. Matthew the Evangelist by Alessio Gimignani, Italy

Matthew spent all of his time with Jesus.

Long after Jesus had died, Matthew wrote down everything he could remember about Jesus' life. His writings became the first of the four gospels.

ST. MATTHEW IS KNOWN AS THE PATRON SAINT OF ACCOUNTANTS, BANKERS, BOOKKEEPERS, AND TAX COLLECTORS. ST. MATTHEW'S FEAST DAY IS SEPTEMBER 21.

St. Matthew the Evangelist by Vincenzo Campi, Italy

St. Mark

Feast Day: April 25

Mark was a companion of the disciples Peter and Paul, and he worked alongside the early missionaries.

Mark lived in the city of Jerusalem where his mother's house was a meeting place for the disciples.

Mark decided to become a missionary and when he arrived in Rome, Italy, he became a close companion of Peter. When Mark wrote his gospel, he shared the stories that Peter had told him about the life and teachings of Jesus.

Saint Mark the Evangelist, unknown artist

Mark gave us special stories of Jesus' life.

Mark's later life is shrouded in legend. In AD 829, his remains were taken to Venice, Italy, where, it is said, they still lie today inside the famous St. Mark's Basilica.

ST. MARK IS KNOWN AS THE PATRON SAINT OF LAWYERS AND NOTARIES. HE'S ALSO THE PATRON SAINT OF VENICE, ITALY, AS WELL AS OTHER PLACES. MARK IS USUALLY SHOWN HOLDING HIS GOSPEL. HIS OTHER SPECIAL SYMBOL IS A WINGED LION.

Woodcut engraving after a drawing by Julius Schnorr von Carolsfeld

St. Luke

Feast Day: October 18

A doctor, a historian, and a fine writer, Luke had many talents. He was the author of the simple but moving account of Jesus' birth that millions of us know today.

Luke was a great writer with a gentle heart.

Luke was a Greek doctor who lived in Antioch. He was baptized by some of the first missionaries several years after Jesus' death and resurrection.

Luke was a friend of Paul and traveled with him on two missionary journeys. When Paul was arrested and sent to Rome, Luke went with him. On the voyage, their ship broke up in stormy seas. With God's help, every crew member managed to swim to shore.

Luke lived to be very old and is believed to have died peacefully in ancient Greece.

Fresco of St. Luke the Evangelist by Giovani Battista Ricci, Italy

ST. LUKE IS THE PATRON SAINT OF MANY THINGS INCLUDING DOCTORS, SURGEONS, CRAFTSPEOPLE, AND ARTISTS. LUKE'S SYMBOL IS AN OX BECAUSE LUKE'S GOSPEL BEGINS WITH ZECHARIAH'S SACRIFICE IN THE TEMPLE. LUKE WROTE THE THIRD GOSPEL AND THE ACTS OF THE APOSTLES.

A painting of a bull, unknown artist, Jerusalem

St. John

Feast Day: December 27

Once a follower of John the Baptist, John left behind a content fisherman's life to become a disciple of Jesus. In later years he wrote down everything he had seen in the Gospel according to St. John.

John and his older brother, James, were successful fishermen in Galilee. But when Jesus called them to become his disciples, they turned their backs on their work.

John spent time with Jesus and became a devoted friend.

Saint John the Evangelist, unknown artist

John was such a valued friend that, moments before Jesus' death, Jesus asked John to take care of his mother, Mary.

John later suffered hardship and imprisonment as he helped to build the Christian church. After traveling in Turkey and Greece, he went to Rome, Italy, where the emperor had him thrown into boiling oil. Miraculously, John survived and was over 90 years old when he died.

IN HIS LAST YEARS, JOHN RETURNED TO TURKEY, WHERE HE WORKED ON HIS GOSPEL. ST. JOHN IS THE PATRON SAINT OF BOOKBINDERS, PRINTERS, THEOLOGIANS, AND WRITERS. HE'S ALSO KNOWN AS THE PATRON SAINT OF LOVE, LOYALTY, AND FRIENDSHIP.

A printing press, unknown artist

The Sermon of St. Stephen by an Italian painter of Venetian School Vittore Carpaccio, Louvre Museum, Paris. France.

St. Stephen

Feast Day: December 26

Stephen was the first Christian martyr—the first person ever to die for the Christian faith. He lived at a time when it was dangerous to be a Christian, and he was sentenced to a brutal death.

Stephen was one of seven people chosen by the apostles to help them spread the message of Jesus and care for the poor.

Stephen was a very special person.

He was a wise and educated man. He gave inspiring talks and encouraged many people to become Christians.

Stephen explained that Jesus had died to save people from their sins and had risen again to show his power over death. He said that people who believed in Jesus would have eternal life. Sadly, Stephen made powerful enemies among the Jewish elders. They did not believe that Jesus was the Messiah, and they argued with Stephen, but he patiently stood his ground. They made up charges against Stephen and took him to the Jewish court.

In the courtroom, Stephen criticized his accusers for not believing in Jesus. Looking up, he told them he could see a vision of Jesus with God in heaven. This angered the court so much that it ordered Stephen to be stoned to death. In this cruel way he became the first Christian martyr.

ST. STEPHEN IS THE PATRON SAINT OF MANY THINGS, SUCH AS BUILDERS, BRICKLAYERS, STONEMASONS, AND DEACONS. HE IS OFTEN SHOWN WITH STONES, THE SYMBOLS OF HIS MARTYRDOM.

St. Sebastian

Feast Day: January 20

Sebastian was a Roman soldier with a deadly secret—he was a Christian. He lived at a time when the emperor, Diocletian, was persecuting Christians.

Sebastian risked his life to help his fellow believers.

While Sebastian appeared to be one of the emperor's loyal guards, secretly he was comforting Christian prisoners and converting prison guards.

The emperor, who admired Sebastian, asked him to be one of his personal bodyguards. But when he discovered Sebastian's true faith, Diocletian was furious and ordered him to be shot with arrows. The execution was carried out and Sebastian was left for dead, but a woman named Irene found him still alive and nursed him back to health.

With great courage Sebastian returned to the emperor and protested against his cruelty. Diocletian ordered him to be clubbed to death. This time Sebastian died of his wounds.

Saint Sebastian by Raphael, Italy

A CHURCH NOW STANDS ON THE SPOT OUTSIDE ROME, ITALY, WHERE SEBASTIAN IS BELIEVED TO BE BURIED. ST. SEBASTIAN IS THE PATRON SAINT OF ARCHERS, ATHLETES, AND SOLDIERS, AS WELL AS MANY OTHER THINGS TOO.

St. Brigid of Kildare

Feast Day: February 1

Brigid is one of the three patron saints of Ireland. Unusually for the time, she founded and headed up a double abbey for nuns and monks.

It is believed that Brigid was born around AD 450 in Leinster, Ireland, to a noble father and enslaved mother. Brigid's father sold her and her mother to a Druid landowner.

At age 10, Brigid was freed and returned to her father, who despised his daughter's charitable nature and tried to sell her to the king of Leinster.

The king was impressed by her compassionate actions.

Saint Brigid of Kildare, unknown artist, Italy

Brigid was removed from her father's guardianship.

Around AD 470, she founded a double monastery in Kildare for monks and nuns. Here, abbesses ranked above abbots. She also went on to set up other nunneries, as well as a school of art.

Cathedral Church of St. Brigid, in Kildare

ON THE EVE OF ST. BRIGID'S FEAST DAY, MANY PEOPLE MAKE A FOUR-ARMED CROSS OUT OF REEDS, RUSHES, OR STRAW, WHICH IS SPRINKLED WITH HOLY WATER. IT IS HUNG IN A HOUSE OR ABOVE THE DOOR TO WELCOME ST. BRIGID. THE CROSSES OFTEN STAY UP PAST THE FEAST DAY TO BENEFIT FROM THE SAINT'S PROTECTION.

St. Thérèse of Lisieux

Feast Day: October 1

In her short life, Thérèse offered small sacrifices rather than great deeds, and was remembered for showing the "little ways" people could be spiritual.

Thérèse was born in 1873 in France and grew up in a religious household. Her four elder sisters all became nuns and she entered the Carmelite convent in Lisieux when she was 15 years old. A strong-willed and stubborn child, by the time she joined the convent she became focused on offering little sacrifices rather than heroic acts to demonstrate her holiness. She thought of herself as a simple, humble wildflower rather than a majestic rose.

Fresco of Glory of St. Thérèse of the Child Jesus by Francisco Labarta, Barcelona, Spain

She became known as The Little Flower.

Thérèse died from tuberculosis at age 24. A year after her death, a collection of her essays was published.

THÉRÈSE SAID THAT AFTER HER DEATH SHE WOULD DO GOOD IN HEAVEN AND WOULD SEND DOWN A "SHOWER OF ROSES" TO EARTH. CATHOLICS DEVOTED TO ST. THÉRÈSE PRAY TO HER AND BELIEVE THAT THEY WILL BE SENT A ROSE FROM HEAVEN. ST. THÉRÈSE IS KNOWN AS THE PATRON SAINT OF MISSIONS, FLORISTS, PILOTS, AND MANY OTHER THINGS.

St. Agnes

Feast Day: January 21

The legend of St. Agnes tells of a young girl who was so devoted to Christ that she decided to never get married. Christians like Agnes faced persecution from the Romans, and her decision cost Agnes her life.

Agnes is believed to have lived in Rome, Italy, around AD 340-350. Many men wanted to marry her. However, Agnes refused them all, stating that Christ had chosen her and she would be his alone. One man who had hoped to marry Agnes was so angry at this refusal that he told the Romans about her. Soon after, Agnes was arrested and ordered to give up her Christian beliefs. She bravely and calmly stood by her faith and chose to be executed instead.

Saint Agnes Outside the Walls (St Agnes has the lamb under her left arm) by Amelia De Angelis, Italy

Roman writers of the time praised Agnes for the incredible courage she showed.

ST. AGNES IS KNOWN AS THE PATRON SAINT OF MANY THINGS, INCLUDING ENGAGED COUPLES, GARDENERS, GIRLS, AND YOUNG WOMEN. IN PAINTINGS, ST. AGNES IS OFTEN SHOWN WITH A LAMB—A SYMBOL OF PURITY AND INNOCENCE. THE NAME AGNES COMES FROM THE LATIN WORD FOR A LAMB, *AGNUS*.

St. Anthony of Padua

Feast Day: June 13

Anthony had a special ability to convey teachings in a simple way so that everyone could understand them. He was greatly admired as a preacher.

Born Fernando Martins in Lisbon, Portugal, in 1195, he joined an Augustine order at the age of 15. In 1220, he joined a Franciscan order and took the name Anthony. On his way to Morocco to spread God's word, Anthony became ill and had to return to Portugal. However, his ship was blown off course and he ended up in Sicily and, eventually, at the San Paolo hermitage in Italy. Here, he studied and became such a moving and expressive preacher that St. Francis of Assisi (pages 40–41) entrusted him with teaching the friars.

Fresco of Apotheosis of St. Anthony of Padua by Gino Terreni, Italy

His preaching was known for clarity and simplicity.

IT IS SAID THAT ONE DAY A NOVICE STOLE ANTHONY'S BOOK OF PSALMS THAT CONTAINED HIS TEACHINGS. ANTHONY PRAYED FOR THE RETURN OF THE BOOK. THE NOVICE BROUGHT THE BOOK BACK AND ALSO RETURNED TO THE FRANCISCAN ORDER HIMSELF. THIS IS HOW ST. ANTHONY BECAME KNOWN AS THE PATRON SAINT OF LOST THINGS.

Anthony of Padua by Giovanni Antonio Galli, Italy.

St. Cecilia

Feast Day: November 22

The story of Cecilia, born in Rome, is little more than legend. Cecilia was said to hear heavenly music whenever she prayed to God. Music brought her strength through dangerous times, and she sang to God for comfort as she faced a cruel death.

At an early age, Cecilia devoted herself to God.

When Cecilia was promised in marriage to a man named Valerian, she was unhappy. She prayed and was comforted by heavenly music. Valerian understood why Cecilia did not want a husband. He respected her wishes and became a Christian, too. At this time, Christians were executed daily by the Roman authorities. When Valerian and his brother Tiburtius were discovered burying these Christian martyrs, they were also executed.

Mosaic of St. Cecilia, Austria

CECILIA NEVER TRIED TO HIDE HER FAITH. SHE PREACHED OPENLY AND CONVERTED PEOPLE TO CHRISTIANITY. IN TIME, SHE WAS ARRESTED AND WAS LATER BEHEADED. SHE IS THE PATRON SAINT OF MANY MUSICAL THINGS, INCLUDING COMPOSERS, MUSIC, MUSICIANS, ORGAN BUILDERS, AND SINGERS.

Mosaic wall decoration of Joan of Arc, Sacré-Cœur Basilica, Paris, France

St. Joan of Arc

Feast Day: May 30

At a time when France was at war with England, a young French girl answered God's call and led her country to victory. She followed her conscience in the face of death and, years later, was made a saint.

Joan of Arc, the youngest daughter of a poor farmer, grew up in a small French village and never learned to read or write. In 1425, at age 13, she began to hear voices who she said were those of saints. They commanded her to drive out the English army from France.

Joan was determined to follow God's will.

She suffered setbacks, but impressed people with her devotion and courage. Charles, the crown prince of France, gave her a small army. In April 1429, at age 17, she led her troops to victory against the English and freed the city of Orléans.

Joan won victory in five more battles. By chance, she was captured and sold to the English. They wanted to get rid of her and charged her with witchcraft. At her trial Joan spoke bravely about her voices and her calling from God, but the English sent her to a terrible death. On May 30, 1431 Joan was burned at the stake in the marketplace in Rouen, France, and her ashes were thrown into the Seine River.

ST. JOAN OF ARC WAS MADE A SAINT 500 YEARS AFTER HER DEATH. SHE IS KNOWN AS THE PATRON SAINT OF FRANCE AND OF SOLDIERS, AS WELL AS MANY THINGS ACROSS DIFFERENT TRADITIONS.

St. Augustine

Feast Day: August 28

St. Augustine is one of the most important figures of the Christian church. He is famous not for the things he did but for the things he thought and wrote.

Augustine was born in North Africa to a Christian mother and a pagan father. He was brought up as a Christian, but as he grew older he lost interest in leading a good life and put aside his Christian faith.

Augustine studied public speaking. When he was around 30, he went to Rome, Italy, and taught there as a professor. Yet he felt something important was missing from his life. He met with priests and bishops and became interested in Christianity again. He was converted very suddenly in his garden one evening after reading some words by St. Paul.

Augustine returned to North Africa and set up a monastery there. For the rest of his life, as a monk, a priest, and the Bishop of Hippo, he preached to people and cared for the poor.

But, most of all, Augustine wrote.

He wrote about his sinful past, his search for God, and about the history and teachings of Christianity.

ST. AUGUSTINE'S WRITINGS HAVE INSPIRED AND HELPED CHRISTIANS FOR MANY HUNDREDS OF YEARS. HE IS KNOWN AS THE PATRON SAINT OF THEOLOGIANS, PRINTERS, AND MANY OTHER THINGS TOO.

Scenes From the Life of Saint Augustine of Hippo, by Master of Saint Augustine, The Met, New York

St. Patrick by Don Giuseppe Melle,
Basilica di Santa Maria Ausiliatrice, Rome, Italy

St. Patrick

Feast Day: March 17

St. Patrick was a humble man who had great energy and enthusiasm. He spent 25 years converting the Irish people to Christianity. He is now a popular and loved Irish saint.

Patrick, first known as Patricius, was born in Roman Great Britain. His father was a Roman citizen, and his grandfather was a Christian priest. Patrick was a teenager when his life took a dramatic turn. He was captured by pirates, taken to Ireland, and sold as an enslaved person. For six years, he worked for an Irish chief, taking care of sheep and pigs. Longing to escape, he prayed to God every day and night.

Eventually, Patrick escaped and boarded a boat to France. There, he had many more adventures before returning home. Patrick trained to become a priest.

Although he was not well educated, he was deeply caring and sincere. His early years had taught him to trust God. In AD 435, Patrick was made Bishop of Ireland. Ireland didn't belong to the Roman Empire, and Christianity was hardly known.

Patrick was a very successful missionary.

He converted Irish chiefs, set up monasteries, and helped to organize the growing church.

ST. PATRICK DIED AROUND AD 461, AND HAS SINCE BECOME A WIDELY-KNOWN AND LOVED PATRON SAINT OF IRELAND. ST. PATRICK'S DAY IS CELEBRATED BY MILLIONS OF PEOPLE AROUND THE WORLD, ON MARCH 17.

St. Thomas Aquinas

Feast Day: January 28

Thomas Aquinas was a large, silent man. He proved to be one of the most important thinkers, writers, and teachers the Christian church has ever known.

Thomas' writings are still studied by many people today.

St. Thomas Aquinas, unknown artist, church Chiesa di San Rocco, Italy

Thomas Aquinas was born into a wealthy Italian family and had a fantastic education. Yet, to the horror of his parents, he decided to become a monk.

As a monk, Thomas continued to study, and his teachers were the best of the age. Soon he was writing and lecturing at universities in Italy and France. His works are masterpieces of clear thinking and powerful arguments–about the Bible and Christian teachings and ideas.

ST. THOMAS AQUINAS WROTE SO MUCH AND WORKED SO HARD THAT HE IS SAID TO HAVE DICTATED HIS IDEAS TO FOUR DIFFERENT SECRETARIES AT ONE TIME! HE IS KNOWN AS THE PATRON SAINT OF ACADEMICS, PHILOSOPHERS, SCHOOLS AND COLLEGES, THEOLOGIANS, AND NUMEROUS OTHER THINGS.

Saints Peter the Martyr and Thomas Aquinas Refute the Heretics by Andrea Di Bonaiuto, Florence

St. Teresa of Avila

Feast Day: October 15

Teresa was a Spanish nun who devoted her life to poverty and prayer. She set up convents all over Spain, and the books and letters she wrote for her nuns are still widely read today.

Teresa was born in Avila, Spain. When she was a teenager, her mother died, and she decided to become a nun. The convent she joined was easygoing, with frequent visitors from town. Teresa longed for a simpler, more disciplined life. She spent hours in deep prayer and began to have holy visions.

Teresa suffered years of poor health. When she recovered, she started a convent away from the distractions of the world. Here, Teresa and her nuns spent many hours alone with God in prayer.

In time, she started 16 more convents.

Fresco of Madonna with the St Teresa of Avila among the angels, Genova, Italy

THOUGH LIFE WAS STRICT, TERESA WAS A WARM, CHEERFUL WOMAN AND WAS GREATLY LOVED BY HER NUNS. SHE WROTE LETTERS OF ENCOURAGEMENT TO THEM ALL, AND HER BOOKS ABOUT A LIFE OF PRAYER ARE STILL INSPIRING TO READ. AMONG MANY OTHER THINGS, ST. TERESA OF AVILA IS KNOWN AS THE PATRON SAINT OF LACE MAKERS.

St. Francis of Assisi

Feast Day: October 4

St. Francis gave up a life of wealth and comfort to help and care for the poor. He is a popular saint, particularly with children, and is fondly remembered for his love of animals and all of God's creations.

Francis lived in Assisi, Italy, and was the son of a wealthy merchant. He was expected to go into the family business, but he was more interested in helping the poor and sick.

His new life was one of poverty and prayer. He traveled, preaching and caring for the sick and living on what people gave him. He devotedly nursed a man with leprosy—an illness greatly feared at the time—and publicly kissed the man's hand. In time, he formed a group of monks known as the Franciscans.

Francis' strength and courage inspired people to follow him.

Toward the end of his life, Francis had a vision of Christ on the cross. When it was over, Francis found that his hands and feet were bleeding, just like the crucified Christ's. These wounds, known as stigmata, lasted until he died.

ST. FRANCIS IS KNOWN AS THE PATRON SAINT OF ANIMALS. IN OCTOBER, ANIMAL BLESSINGS ARE OFTEN HELD AROUND THE WORLD IN HONOR OF ST. FRANCIS AND HIS LOVE FOR NATURE. DURING THE BLESSING CEREMONY, HOLY WATER MAY BE SPRINKLED ON PETS AND OTHER ANIMALS, AND PEOPLE PRAY FOR THEM. ST. FRANCIS IS ALSO THE PATRON SAINT OF ECOLOGISTS AND OF ITALY.

Sermon to the Birds by Giotto,
Umbria, Italy

St. Elizabeth of Hungary

Feast Day: November 17

For most of her short life, Elizabeth knew only wealth and happiness. When that happiness came to a sudden end, she turned her back on her comfortable life, and devoted herself to the poor.

Elizabeth was compassionate, and very generous to the poor.

Elizabeth was daughter of the king of Hungary. When she was only four years old, she was engaged to a prince named Louis, and sent to live in Germany. Elizabeth grew up to love Louis. Years later they married and had three children.

When Louis suddenly died of the plague, Elizabeth was heartbroken. She was thrown out of her home by Louis' brother and joined a Franciscan order of nuns.

She then lived a life of poverty, helping the poor and sick. She was beaten by her spiritual teacher, which made her weak and ill. She died when she was only 24.

St. Elizabeth of Hungary by *Marin Janchini*, in church Chiesa dei Cappuccini, Italy

ST. ELIZABETH WAS A ROYAL PRINCESS, AND HER CROWN HAS BECOME HER SYMBOL. SHE IS KNOWN AS THE PATRON SAINT OF MANY THINGS, INCLUDING BAKERS, CHARITIES, AND LACE MAKERS.

St. Rose of Lima

Feast Day: August 23

St. Rose was the first saint of the Americas. This beautiful young woman was not interested in marriage. Instead, she lived a life of holiness and hardship and dedicated herself to God.

Rose was the daughter of a Spanish family who lived in Lima, Peru. She hated her beauty.

Rose had many admirers, but she decided to become a nun.

She lived in a hut in her garden at home, and led a life that she believed would bring her closer to God. She spent many hours praying. She wore a crown of roses that dug their thorns into her head, and a dress made of the roughest cloth. She fasted several times each week and would not drink to quench her thirst. Sadly, she became weak and died aged 31.

The *Mystic Marriage* of St Rose of Lima, attributed to Lazzaro Baldi, Italy

HUGE CROWDS LINED THE STREETS AT ST. ROSE OF LIMA'S FUNERAL, AND HER HOME HAS BECOME A SHRINE. THE ROSE IS LINKED WITH ST. ROSE'S NAME AND HAS BECOME HER SYMBOL. SHE IS KNOWN AS THE PATRON SAINT OF FLORISTS, GARDENERS, PERU, SOUTH AMERICA, AND NUMEROUS OTHER THINGS TOO.

St. Nicholas

Feast Day: December 6

Legend tells us that St. Nicholas was a sweet, kind, generous man who liked to help people in need. He is known around the world as "Santa Claus" and is one of the most popular saints.

We know very little about St. Nicholas. He was a bishop who lived in Myra, Turkey, at some time during the AD 300s. There are many different stories about him. In one, he is said to have helped three young sisters who were too poor to marry. Nicholas threw three bags of gold through their window at night. This was a secret, generous act that asked for nothing in return.

Painting of St Nicholas, unknown artist

Stories about St. Nicholas have spread around the world.

The name "Claus" evolved from the Dutch name for St. Nicholas.

TODAY ST. NICHOLAS HAS BECOME THE SECRET VISITOR WHO LEAVES PRESENTS FOR GOOD CHILDREN. IN SOME COUNTRIES, CHILDREN RECEIVE PRESENTS ON HIS FEAST DAY; IN OTHERS, ON CHRISTMAS EVE. HE IS CONSIDERED THE PATRON SAINT OF MANY COUNTRIES, SUCH AS RUSSIA AND GREECE. HE'S ALSO THE PATRON SAINT OF CHILDREN, MERCHANTS, SAILORS, AND MUCH MORE.

St. Bernadette

Feast Day: April 16

Bernadette was a poor girl from Lourdes, France, who had visions of the Virgin Mary. These have made her hometown an important place of Christian pilgrimage.

Bernadette was quiet and humble and did not enjoy attention.

Bernadette was only 14 years old when she had a vision of the Virgin Mary. Over the next six months, she had many more. In the visions, Mary spoke to Bernadette, led her to a spring of healing water, and asked her to build a church.

Priests were suspicious about Bernadette's visions and questioned her for many years. She stood by her story and was finally believed. A church was built on the site of her visions, and it was said that the nearby spring was a place of healing.

Appearance of Virgin Mary to St. Bernadette, by A. Nicolas, Lourdes, France

ST. BERNADETTE ENTERED A CONVENT, WHERE SHE WORKED AND PRAYED. SHE HAD ALWAYS SUFFERED FROM POOR HEALTH AND WAS ONLY 35 WHEN SHE DIED. LOURDES REMAINS A VERY IMPORTANT PLACE FOR MANY, AND MILLIONS OF PEOPLE TRAVEL THERE EACH YEAR. ST. BERNADETTE IS KNOWN AS THE PATRON SAINT OF MANY THINGS, INCLUDING SHEPHERDS AND SHEPHERDESSES.

St. Teresa of Calcutta

Feast Day: September 5

Teresa wanted to become a missionary from a young age. Throughout her life, she set up the Missionaries of Charity, as well as many hospices and orphanages.

In 1928, when Teresa was 18 years old, she went to Ireland, joining a group that had missions in India. The following year she traveled to Calcutta and in 1931 became a nun. While teaching in Calcutta, she was deeply troubled by the poverty she witnessed. In 1950, she set up the Missionaries of Charity, whose aim was to help:

people who felt unwanted, unloved, uncared for.

Fresco of Padre Pio and Mother Teresa, unknown artist, Valencia, Spain

Teresa set up hospices and orphanages in India and around the world. Throughout her life, Teresa struggled with her faith, often experiencing doubts. However, she continued her great and long service to others and God.

ST. TERESA DIED IN 1977. SHE WAS MORE COMMONLY KNOWN AS MOTHER TERESA, TAKING ON THAT NAME WHEN SHE TOOK HER FINAL PROFESSION OF VOWS. SHE WAS USUALLY SEEN WEARING A WHITE SARI WITH A BLUE BORDER, THE HABIT OF THE MISSIONARIES OF CHARITY. SHE IS KNOWN AS THE PATRON SAINT OF WORLD YOUTH DAY AND MANY OTHER THINGS TOO.

St. Carlo Acutis

Feast Day: October 12

Carlo used his interest in computers to create a website detailing global miracles, which was used by parishes from around the world. In this way, he helped spread God's word.

Born in 1991, Carlo grew up in Italy with his family. A caring boy, he loved to help others and became interested in Catholicism from a young age.

Carlo used modern methods to help people understand the gospel.

Carlo was fascinated by computers, from gaming to programming. At age 11, he started documenting eucharistic miracles throughout history, creating a database that listed when miracles occurred and in what country.

He was only 15 years old when he died from leukemia. Since his death, various miracles have been linked to him.

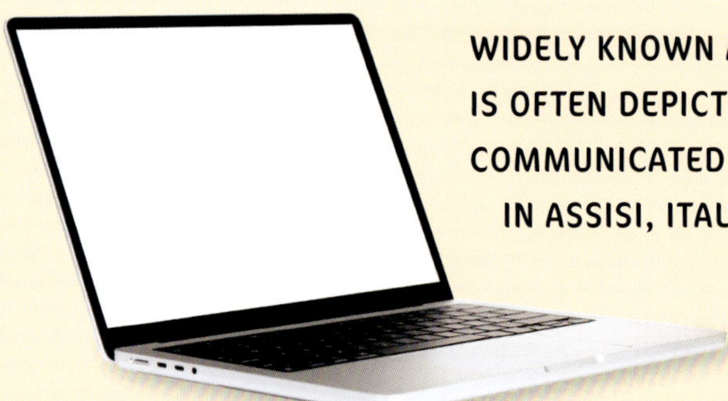

WIDELY KNOWN AS THE "FIRST MILLENNIAL SAINT", CARLO IS OFTEN DEPICTED WITH A COMPUTER, SHOWING HOW HE COMMUNICATED HIS MESSAGE TO THE WORLD. IN AUGUST 2025, IN ASSISI, ITALY, A SCULPTURE OF ST. CARLO KNEELING BESIDE CHRIST WITH A LAPTOP IN HIS HAND WAS UNVEILED. HE'S KNOWN AS THE PATRON SAINT OF COMPUTER PROGRAMMERS.

Annunciation to the Shepherds, woodcut engraving after a drawing by Julius Schnorr von Carolsfeld

What are angels?

Feast Day: September 29 (all angels)

Angels are God's messengers. In the Bible, these beautiful beings are sent from heaven to people on Earth to deliver help, warnings, or exciting news.

Angels are a link between heaven and Earth.

In the Bible, angels appear in different ways. Sometimes they appear in a blaze of glory, dazzling onlookers and filling them with fear. This is how the angels appeared to the shepherds in Bethlehem on the night that Jesus was born. Angels sometimes appear to people while they are asleep. An angel appeared in Joseph's dreams to tell him that Mary was expecting the Son of God. At other times, angels take a human form. In the Old Testament, Abraham meets three strangers, whom he invites into his tent for a meal. It is only when they tell him that his wife, Sarah, will have a child that he realizes they are really angels.

Angels deliver important messages and also provide practical help. They protect those who show obedience to God; in the Old Testament, an angel protects Daniel when he is thrown into a lions' den. They also protect those who do God's work; in the New Testament, an angel frees Peter from prison by breaking his chains.

ANGELS ARE HOLY BEINGS THAT WERE CREATED BY GOD AND HAVE DIRECT CONTACT WITH THE CREATOR. THE BIBLE TELLS US THAT ANGELS WORSHIP ONLY GOD. THEY ARE HAPPY WHEN PEOPLE COME TO KNOW AND LOVE GOD. IN FACT, WHEN HUMANS DIE, ANGELS ARE SAID TO CARRY THEM INTO HEAVEN.

A Renaissance fresco

Guardian angels

Some Christians believe that, at the moment of our birth, each of us is given a guardian angel to accompany us through life. This comforting idea has existed for many thousands of years and is even mentioned in the Bible.

Some Christians believe that guardian angels are always there to help and protect us.

They are our partners on the path to heaven.

When Peter the apostle is thrown into prison by Herod Antipas, his fellow Christians pray for his safety. These prayers are heard by God, who sends an angel to the prison. The angel removes Peter's chains. At first, Peter thinks it is all a dream, but when the angel leads him to freedom, he realizes the angel was sent by God to deliver him from Herod.

The Liberation Of Saint Peter by Domenichino, Chiesa di San Pletro in Vincoli, Italy

THE FEAST DAY OF THE GUARDIAN ANGELS IS ON OCTOBER 2 EACH YEAR. MANY PEOPLE BELIEVE THAT GUARDIAN ANGELS HELP US WITH SPIRITUAL GROWTH. PEOPLE MAY CALL ON ANGELS TO PROTECT THEM IN THEIR STRUGGLE TO LEAD GOOD LIVES.

A guardian angel, unknown artist, Chiesa di San Francesco

Choirs of angels

Countless angels are said to exist in heaven. Christians have attempted to sort these heavenly beings into different groups. Some groups of angels had specific roles, and were said to perform particular tasks.

The highest group are the archangels.

Only three archangels–Michael, Gabriel, and Raphael–are named in the Bible, even though Raphael says he is one of seven. The archangels are powerful beings who are very close to God and have the authority to bring about great change.

Two other groups of angels are the cherubim and seraphim. They are said to surround and worship the throne of heaven and to serve God day and night. The Book of Genesis tells us that when Adam and Eve were banished from the Garden of Eden, God sent the cherubim to guard the Tree of Life.

The Expulsion of Adam and Eve From Paradise, by Julius Schnorr von Carolsfeld

THERE IS AN IMPORTANT DIFFERENCE BETWEEN THE ARCHANGELS AND THE CHERUBIM AND SERAPHIM. ARCHANGELS HAVE CONTACT WITH PEOPLE ON EARTH; CHERUBIM AND SERAPHIM DO NOT.

Archangel Michael

Feast Day: September 29

Michael is God's most trusted creature and carries out heaven's commands. He is a fierce warrior, protector, and comforting guardian.

Michael is heaven's most powerful archangel.

In the Old Testament, Daniel says he believes Michael to be the guardian of the Israelites. The very name, Michael, means "who is like God"—a good name for an angel who acts with great authority, almost as an assistant to God.

Michael is a champion of goodness and justice and fights evil at every chance. When one of God's angels, Lucifer, started a war in heaven (see pages 58–59), Michael fought and defeated the rebels and threw them out of heaven. No wonder Michael is known as the warrior angel.

There are several legends about Michael. It is said that this angel appeared in Rome, Italy, when there was a horrible plague. This may be why Michael is said to protect the sick and receive their souls into heaven. Michael is also believed to be a guardian of high places. Two monasteries dedicated to Michael—St. Michael's Mount in Great Britain and Mont St. Michel in France—were both built on outcrops of rock.

ARCHANGEL MICHAEL'S FEAST DAY IS KNOWN AS THE FEAST DAY OF "ST. MICHAEL AND ALL THE ANGELS." HE IS KNOWN AS THE PATRON SAINT OF BRUSSELS, BELGIUM, AND OF POLICE OFFICERS AND IS OFTEN SHOWN WEARING A FULL SUIT OF ARMOR. HE'S ALSO KNOWN AS THE PATRON SAINT, GUARDIAN, AND PROTECTOR OF NUMEROUS OTHER THINGS AS WELL.

St Michael the Archangel, Ludovico Gimignani
Chapel of St Michael the Archangel, Basilica di Sant Andrea delle Fratte, Rome, Italy.

The Annunciation by Philippe de Champaigne, The Met, New York
The archangel Gabriel told Mary her child would be the Son of God

Archangel Gabriel

Feast Day: September 29

The archangel Gabriel is one of the best known of all the angels. It was Gabriel who appeared to Mary and told her the exciting news that she was to have a baby, who would be the Son of God.

Gabriel is mentioned several times in the Bible, and he is always the bringer of important news.

In the Old Testament, Gabriel appears to Daniel in the form of a man. Gabriel helps Daniel understand a puzzling vision and prophesies the coming of Jesus.

In the New Testament, Gabriel appears to Zechariah, and tells him that he will have a son named John who will grow up to be a great prophet–the famous John the Baptist. Zechariah is so frightened that he is speechless with shock! A few months later, God sends Gabriel to tell Mary about the birth of Jesus –the Son of God.

Annunciation, by Giovanni Battista Salvi-Sassoferrato, Basilica di San Pietro

MANY ARTISTS HAVE PAINTED THE SCENE WHERE GABRIEL TELLS MARY ABOUT THE BIRTH OF JESUS. THIS IS KNOWN AS THE ANNUNCIATION. THE NAME GABRIEL MEANS "THE HERO OF GOD." ARCHANGEL GABRIEL IS KNOWN AS THE PATRON SAINT OF MANY THINGS, INCLUDING BROADCASTERS, MESSENGERS, POSTAL WORKERS, AND WRITERS.

Archangel Raphael

Feast Day: September 29

The name Raphael means "God heals." There is a story about this caring archangel showing a young man called Tobias how to heal his father's blindness.

Tobit, who lived long before Jesus was born, was a good man who helped the poor. But one night he suddenly lost his sight. His blindness was a burden to him, and he prayed to God to let him die. God heard his prayers and sent Raphael to help.

Meanwhile Tobit was preparing for death. He asked his son, Tobias, to collect some savings from a place called Media. Raphael appeared to Tobias in human form, explained that he was a distant relative, and went with him.

One day Tobias caught a fish. Raphael told him to remove its insides, which he said could be used for healing.

Weeks later, when the travelers returned home, Raphael told Tobias to rub the fish on his father's eyes.

Miraculously, Tobit's blindness was healed!

Raphael revealed his true identity, stating he was one of the seven holy angels. The angel told Tobit and Tobias to praise and thank God, before vanishing and returning to heaven.

ARCHANGEL RAPHAEL IS KNOWN AS THE PATRON SAINT OF NUMEROUS THINGS, INCLUDING DOCTORS, NURSES, PEOPLE WHO ARE BLIND, AND TRAVELERS. HE IS OFTEN ASSOCIATED WITH HEALING.

Woodcut engraving after a statue by Hermann Schievelbein

Detail of painting of Tobias and archangel Raphael, by Matteo Desiderato, Italy

The Three Archangels by Marco d'Oggiono,
Milan, Italy

Fallen angels

The Bible mentions only four angels by name—Michael, Gabriel, Raphael, and Lucifer. In the beginning, they were all created good, but one of them, Lucifer, was tempted into sin and became God's enemy.

There is a famous story about the angel Lucifer, whose name means "light bearer." Lucifer was very, very proud. In time, this angel wanted to sit on the throne of heaven and enjoy the power that belonged to God alone. Lucifer must have been very persuasive—soon, one third of all the angels agreed to join the rebel angel in the fight against God.

This is how war broke out in heaven.

Small parts of this story appear in old translations of the Bible in the Book of Revelation; others have been added by writers over the years. The story goes that the archangel Michael fought Lucifer and the rebel army and, acting on God's will, threw them out of heaven. At this point in the story, Lucifer was given a new name—Satan. The fallen archangel was chained up in a dark pit for one thousand years. Satan is also now known by other names too.

SATAN TRIED TO TEMPT PEOPLE AWAY FROM GOD IN SEVERAL BIBLE STORIES. WHEN JESUS WENT INTO THE WILDERNESS FOR 40 DAYS AND NIGHTS, SATAN ENCOURAGED HIM TO CHALLENGE GOD AND USE HIS POWER FOR HIS OWN PURPOSES. LATER, SATAN TEMPTED JESUS' DISCIPLE, JUDAS, TO BETRAY HIS MASTER FOR 30 PIECES OF SILVER.

Calendar of feast days

* indicates the saints featured in this book

January

2 St Basil the Great 12 St Benedict 14 St Sava 17 St Anthony Abbot 19 St Henry of Uppsalla 20 *St Sebastian 21 *St Agnes 24 St Francis de Sales 28 *St Thomas Aquinas 31 St John Bosco

February

1 *St Brigid 3 St Anskar 8 St Jerome Emilian 9 St Apollonia 14 St Cyril St Methodius St Valentine 23 St Polycarp

March

1 St David of Wales 2 St Chad 17 *St Patrick 19 *St Joseph 20 St Cuthbert 24 St Iranaeus, Bishop of Sirmium

April

4 St Isidore 11 St Stanislaus 16 *St Bernadette 17 St Stephen Harding 23 St George St Adalbert of Prague 25 *St Mark 29 St Catherine of Siena 30 St Pius V

May

19 St Dunstan 27 St Augustine, Archbishop of Canterbury 30 *St Joan of Arc

June

2 St Erasmus (Elmo) 5 St Boniface 9 St Columba 11 St Barnabus 13 *St Anthony of Padua 22 St Alban 24 *St John the Baptist 28 St Irenaeus, Bishop of Lyons 29 *St Paul *St Peter

July

3 *St Thomas 11 St Benedict 15 St Bonaventure 20 St Margaret of Antioch
22 *St Mary Magdalene 23 St Bridget of Sweden 25 St Christopher St James the Great
26 *St Anne St Joachim 29 St Olaf 31 St Ignatius of Loyola

August

8 St Dominic 10 St Lawrence 11 St Clare 14 St Maximilian Kolbe 15 *Virgin Mary
16 St Stephen of Hungary 20 St Bernard 21 St Pius X 23 *St Rose of Lima 24 St Bartholomew
26 St Ninian 28 *St Augustine, Bishop of Hippo

September

1 St Giles 3 St Gregory the Great 5 *St Teresa of Calcutta 9 St Peter Claver 13 St John Chrysostom 17 St Hildegard 21 *St Matthew 28 St Wenceslaus 29 All angels 30 St Jerome

October

1 *St Thérèse of Lisieux 4 *St Francis of Assisi 6 St Bruno 9 St Denis 10 St Francis Borgia
12 *St Carlo Acutis 13 St Edward the Confessor 15 *St Teresa of Avila 16 St Gall 18 *St Luke
19 St Isaac Jogues 25 St Crispin 28 St Jude St Simon

November

1 All Saints' Day 7 St Willibrord 11 St Martin of Tours 15 St Albert the Great
16 St Margaret of Scotland 17 *St Elizabeth of Hungary 22 *St Cecilia 23 St Clement I
25 St Catherine of Alexandria 30 *St Andrew

December

1 St Edmund Campion 3 St Francis Xavier 4 St Barbara 6 *St Nicholas 7 St Ambrose
10 St Gregory III 13 St Lucy 19 St Anastasius I 26 *St Stephen 27 *St John the Apostle
29 St Thomas à Becket

Glossary

anoint to pour oil over someone or something to make it holy

apostle one who is sent with the authority of Jesus, such as the twelve disciples and St Paul

ascension Jesus' return to heaven after he had been raised from the dead

baptize to use water as a sign of faith, repentance, and sin washed away, admitting the believer to the Christian church

crucifixion a form of execution in which a person is fastened to a wooden cross

disciple anyone who follows and learns from another, such as one of the twelve close followers of Jesus

eternal something that is everlasting, without beginning or end

exile the banishment of someone from their own country

Gospel one of the first four books of the New Testament, which narrate Jesus' life

heaven the place where God and his angels live, and where Christian believers will join God after death

martyr someone who is ready to suffer and die for his or her faith

miracles dramatic and surprising events that cannot be explained

missionaries people who are sent to teach others about their religion

pagan a person with no religious beliefs or who worships different gods

persecution the unfair and cruel treatment of people because of their religion

pilgrimage a journey to a shrine or other holy place

plague an infectious disease that spreads quickly and kills many people

prophet someone who receives messages from God and tells other people about them

resurrection Jesus' return from death to a new life that would last forever

shrine a place that is especially holy–for example, the tomb of a saint

theology the study of religious ideas

visions revelations from God that show events that have not yet happened

Notable people

Abraham	The man chosen by God to be the father of many nations.
Barnabas	A friend and fellow missionary of St Paul and St Mark.
Daniel	An exiled Jew who worked in the royal court of Babylon. He was thrown into a lions' den because of his religion, but an angel was sent to protect him.
Diocletian	Roman emperor (AD 284-305) who ordered the persecution of the Christians.
Elizabeth	The wife of Zechariah and mother of John the Baptist.
Herod (the Great)	The king of Judea when Jesus was born, who ordered all the baby boys to be killed.
Herod Antipas	One of the sons of Herod the Great. He persecuted many Christians and ordered the beheading of John the Baptist.
Herodias	The wife of Herod Antipas, she wanted the head of John the Baptist.
Joachim	The husband of Anne, mother of Mary.
Judas	One of Jesus' twelve disciples. Judas betrayed Jesus to the Romans, leading to Jesus' arrest and death.
Maxentius	Roman emperor (AD 306-312) who ordered the persecution of the Christians.
Salome	The daughter of Herodias. Her dance for Herod Antipas led to the death of John the Baptist.
Sarah	The wife of Abraham.
Tobias	The son of Tobit, who was accompanied on a journey by the archangel Raphael, and helped to cure his father's blindness.
Tobit	The father of Tobias, who became blind and was cured by the archangel Raphael.
Zechariah	The father of John the Baptist.

Index